This book belongs to:

.....................................................................

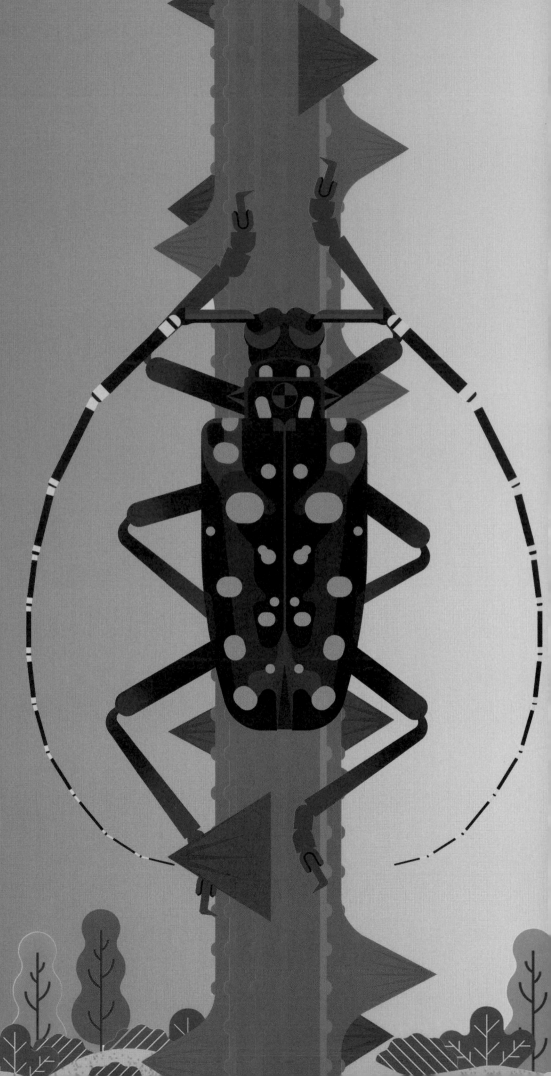

 **DK** | Penguin Random House

**Editor** Sophie Parkes
**Project Art Editors** Polly Appleton, Jaileen Kaur
**Acquisitions Editor** Fay Evans
**Managing Art Editor** Romi Chakraborty
**US Senior Editor** Shannon Beatty
**Production Editor** Rob Dunn
**Production Controller** Isabell Schart
**Jacket Designer** Dheeraj Arora
**Deputy Art Director** Mabel Chan
**Publishing Director** Sarah Larter

**Consultant** Professor Michael Ritchie
**Proofreader and indexer** Susie Rae

Originally published in 2020 by Mosquito Books Barcelona

First American Edition, 2021
Published in the United States by DK Publishing
1450 Broadway, Suite 801, New York, NY 10018

Text © 2020 Lucas Riera
Illustrations © 2020 Ángel Svoboda
© 2020 Mosquito Books Barcelona
21 22 23 24 25  10 9 8 7 6 5 4 3 2 1
001–325276–Sep/2021

A catalog record for this book is available from
the Library of Congress.
ISBN: 978-0-7440-4410-2

DK books are available at special discounts when purchased
in bulk for sales promotions, premiums, fund-raising, or
educational use. For details, contact: DK Publishing Special
Markets, 1450 Broadway, Suite 801, New York, NY 10018
SpecialSales@dk.com

Printed and bound in China

For the curious
**www.dk.com**

MIX
Paper from
responsible sources
FSC™ C018179

# EVOLVED

Lucas Riera · Ángel Svoboda

# In this book you will find...

# Introduction

Evolution is a process that has taken place over thousands of years. However, we sometimes talk about it as if it is now over—as if, though evolution can explain why any given species is the way it is today, the same species won't continue changing and adapting in the future. Evolution is an idea put forward by scientists such as Charles Darwin about how living things adapt (change) during their time on Earth. It's sometimes a difficult idea to understand, though, because we aren't usually able to see it happening before our eyes.

So, what is evolution? You might find it useful to think of it as a never-ending fashion show with all living things walking down a catwalk. The evolution catwalk is full of different feathers, paws, legs, patterns, and colors. The features that are useful and improve an animal's chance of survival in some way, get to continue to walk on the catwalk. However, the features that are less helpful or don't serve a purpose are made to leave the catwalk.

This is evolution: a never-ending experiment where the best of each species survives and thrives in their environment long enough to pass their features onto the next generation.

This book talks about the different features of many animals, and explains how these features affect why some animals survive and some don't. Essentially, evolution means that the features that have continued to exist in animals have done so because they help to improve something that the animals need to do to live, such as hunting, flying, spotting food, roaring, running, or swimming. Basically, any feature that helps animals to survive stays on the catwalk.

If owls were not able to rotate their neck up to 270° to scan the ground and fly without making a sound, they may not have gotten enough to eat to survive. Their prey could have heard them swooping and run away. If giraffes didn't have such long necks, they wouldn't be able to reach their food high in the trees and would have died out. If golden eagles had to close their eyes to protect them from the wind when diving at speeds of up to 150 mph (320 kph), they would crash or not be able to see their prey, and would die. A specially evolved see-through eyelid protects their eyes as they zoom toward their prey. There are endless examples of incredible evolution.

Like clothes on a catwalk, what is fashionable today is not necessarily what people will wear in the future. Other items will be designed that fit better or use improved fabrics that keep us warm in the winter and cool in the summer. In a similar way, more flexible paws, eyes that can see farther into the distance, or legs that can run faster, will replace older designs of these features in animals. This process hasn't finished—it is always happening. Animals as we know them today will continue to change and improve forever.

Welcome to the wonderful world of evolution and adaptation!

LR

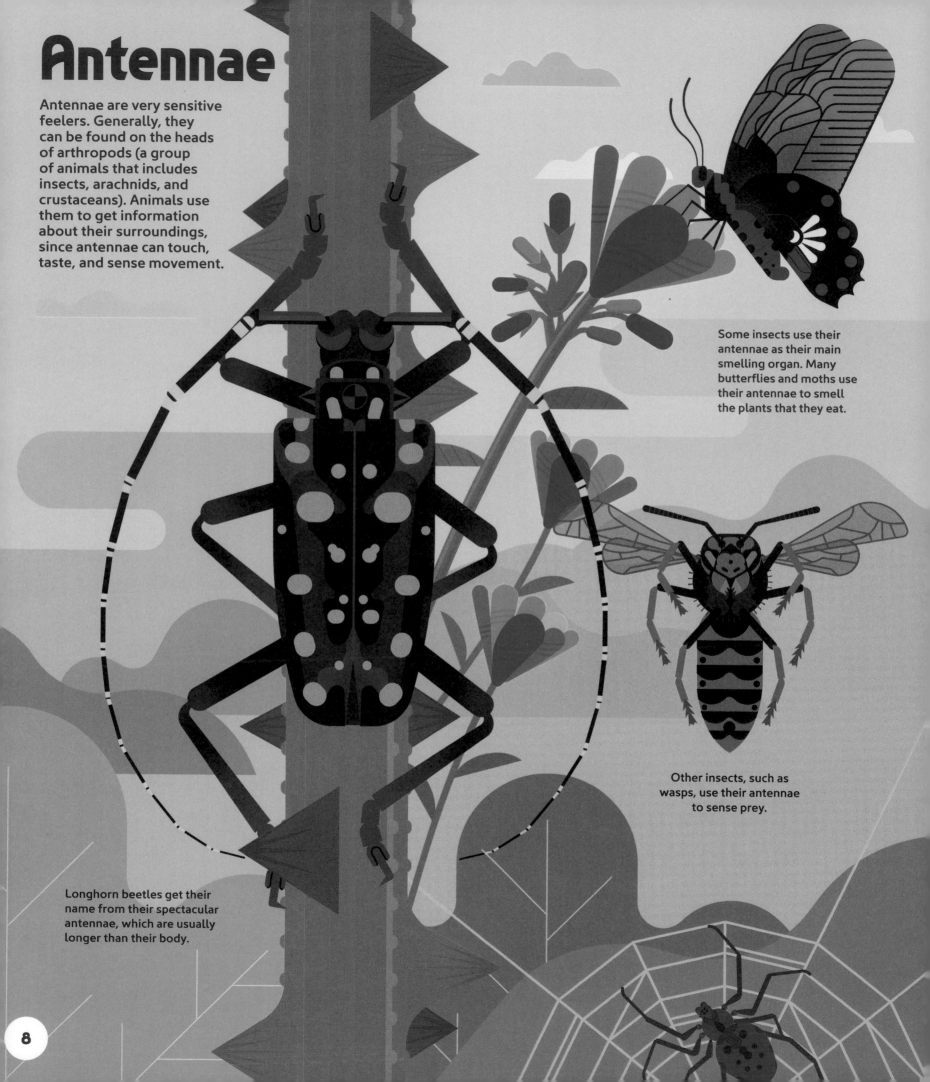

# Antennae

Antennae are very sensitive feelers. Generally, they can be found on the heads of arthropods (a group of animals that includes insects, arachnids, and crustaceans). Animals use them to get information about their surroundings, since antennae can touch, taste, and sense movement.

Some insects use their antennae as their main smelling organ. Many butterflies and moths use their antennae to smell the plants that they eat.

Other insects, such as wasps, use their antennae to sense prey.

Longhorn beetles get their name from their spectacular antennae, which are usually longer than their body.

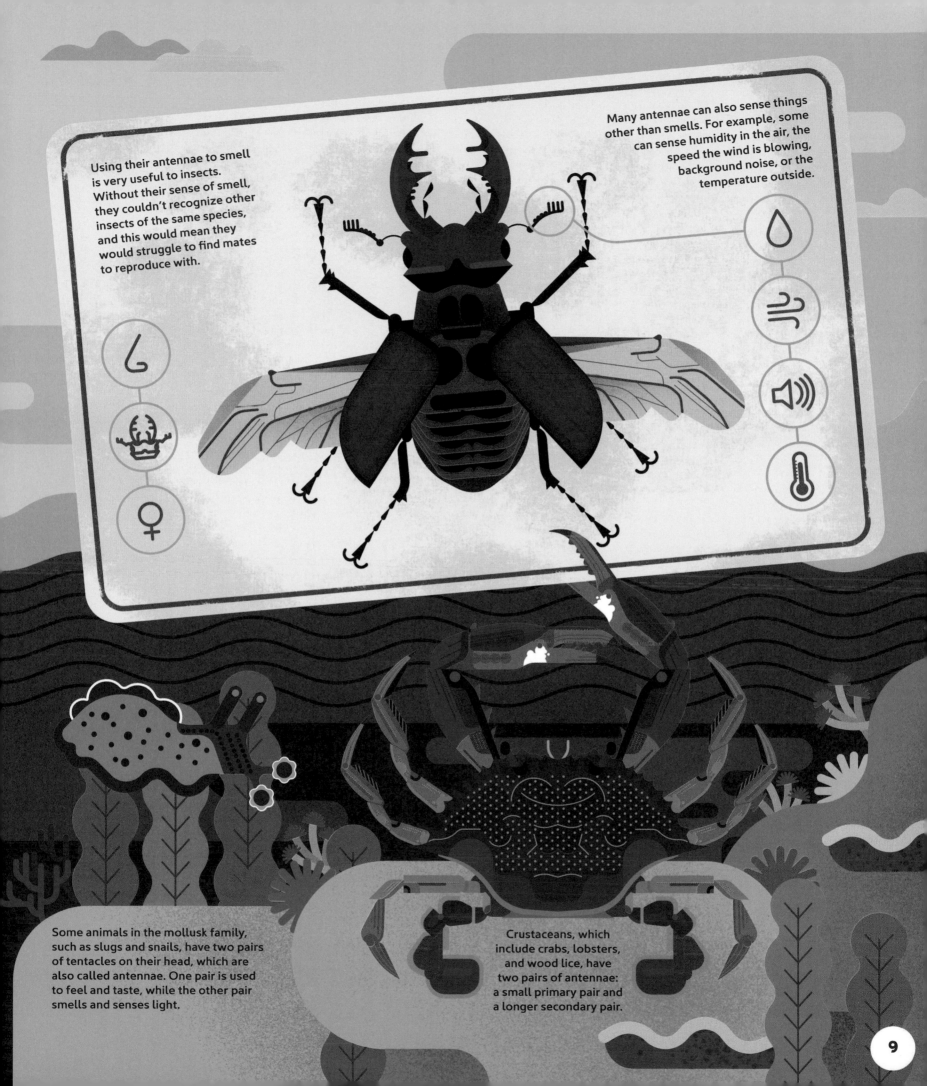

Using their antennae to smell is very useful to insects. Without their sense of smell, they couldn't recognize other insects of the same species, and this would mean they would struggle to find mates to reproduce with.

Many antennae can also sense things other than smells. For example, some can sense humidity in the air, the speed the wind is blowing, background noise, or the temperature outside.

Some animals in the mollusk family, such as slugs and snails, have two pairs of tentacles on their head, which are also called antennae. One pair is used to feel and taste, while the other pair smells and senses light.

Crustaceans, which include crabs, lobsters, and wood lice, have two pairs of antennae: a small primary pair and a longer secondary pair.

# Eyes

The eyes of most animals are highly sophisticated systems—they sense light, adjust their lens, build an image, and turn it into electric signals that the brain receives. Eyes also adapt to the needs of each species.

Octopuses and squid have very large eyes in relation to their bodies. The eyes focus on the images they see by moving the lens closer or farther from the retina (the part of the eye that receives light), just like fish do.

Some animals don't have any eyes at all! This includes fish living in the depths of the ocean, or microscopic animals that live in caves. They don't have eyes because they don't need them at all—they live in complete darkness!

Many animals, such as chameleons, can move each eye separately from the other.

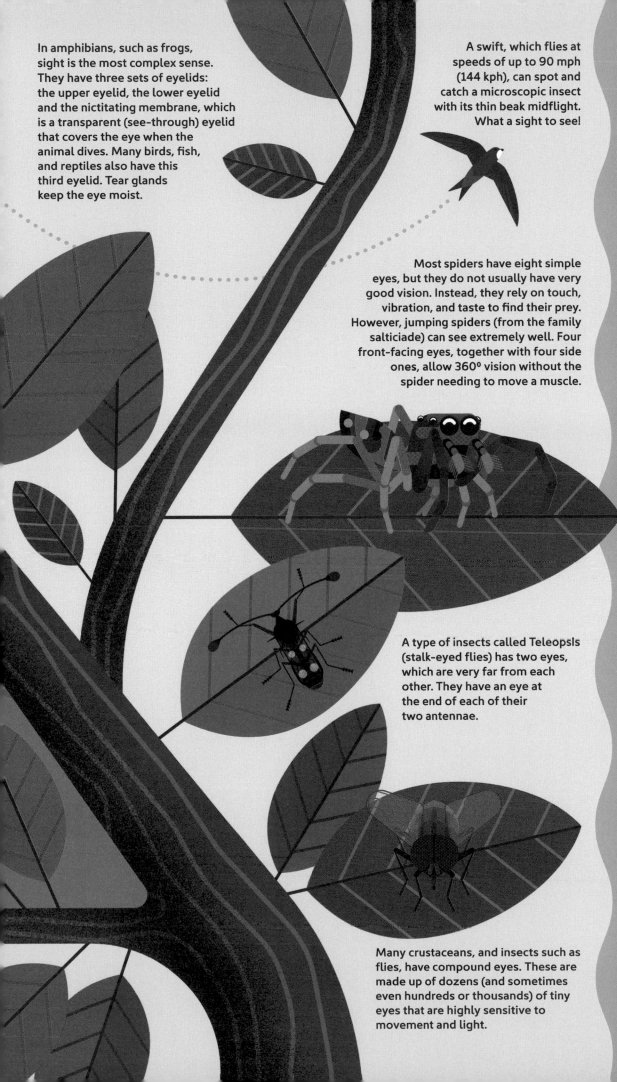

In amphibians, such as frogs, sight is the most complex sense. They have three sets of eyelids: the upper eyelid, the lower eyelid and the nictitating membrane, which is a transparent (see-through) eyelid that covers the eye when the animal dives. Many birds, fish, and reptiles also have this third eyelid. Tear glands keep the eye moist.

A swift, which flies at speeds of up to 90 mph (144 kph), can spot and catch a microscopic insect with its thin beak midflight. What a sight to see!

Most spiders have eight simple eyes, but they do not usually have very good vision. Instead, they rely on touch, vibration, and taste to find their prey. However, jumping spiders (from the family salticiade) can see extremely well. Four front-facing eyes, together with four side ones, allow 360º vision without the spider needing to move a muscle.

A type of insects called Teleopsls (stalk-eyed flies) has two eyes, which are very far from each other. They have an eye at the end of each of their two antennae.

Many crustaceans, and insects such as flies, have compound eyes. These are made up of dozens (and sometimes even hundreds or thousands) of tiny eyes that are highly sensitive to movement and light.

# Do all animals see colors like us?

Not all of them! It can be difficult to picture how other animals might see, but we'll try to explain...

First, let's look at the structures in our eyes that help us see a range of colors. These are called photoreceptors, which are made up of cones—cells found in the retina that perceive color—and rods, cells that help us see in the dark.

Humans see three colors: red, green, and blue (and the colors they make when combined). However, some animals also see ultraviolet—a type of light that is invisible to humans. For example, pigeons are pentachromatic—they can see five colors.

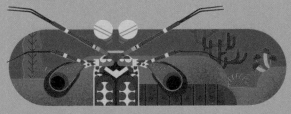

Let's make it even more complicated! Can you imagine your vision if you were a mantis shrimp (stematopoda) and had 12 photoreceptors? They have the most complex eyes in the animal kingdom!

Other animals (usually nocturnal ones, such as owls, or animals that live in dark places), can only see two colors: black and white. However, they may have developed other improved senses, such as hearing or smell, to help them in the dark.

# Fast evolution

## Incredible cases

Changes happen to living things when a part of their DNA (the chemical that their genes are made of) mutates (changes). This can lead to species developing features that are good for them, and those features, called adaptations, remain. However, if a change causes features to develop that are harmful for a species, that species will adapt or slowly die out.

For example, a mutation that results in a change in the color of an animal might mean that it is camouflaged and can hide from predators. Animals of this color are less likely to get eaten, and so they will be able to reproduce and will keep being born with this feature. Most of the time, this process, where each living thing develops its body parts into the best tools to adapt and survive, takes place over hundreds and thousands of years. Evolution is usually slow and undetectable in the short run—but not always, as the examples on this page show.

In 1996, a tropical area in Brazil was flooded by humans to create a reservoir. The flood meant that more than 300 small islands were left in the reservoir.

Many lizards died because their source of food had vanished in the flood. However, one type of tiny gecko managed to survive and evolved incredibly fast—over 15 years, the head of this species grew much bigger.

Why did this happen?

The termite insects that lived on other islands and used to be eaten by bigger lizards could now become the little gecko's source of food. But the gecko's mouth had to be big enough to eat them.

Another example of fast evolution involves salmon in Lake Washington in Washington State. The salmon were introduced into the lake in 1930, but in only 60 years, they had evolved into two different groups. One group lived close to the shore, and the other lived in the depths of the lake. Both groups had remarkable changes in their bodies and DNA after only 15 generations. They evolved to live in new habitats and separated into two types better suited to each habitat. This process can eventually lead to new species.

# Fossils

## Our history picture book

Fossils are ancient remains of animals or plants that have turned into rock. This process is known as petrification. Fossils give us information about the past. They can be made from bone fragments, whole skeletons, or even remains of softer parts of an animal or plant that were squashed onto a rock and can still be seen. Think of fossils as picture books that show us history.

If it weren't for fossils, we could never have known that 100 million years ago the Earth was inhabited by amazing creatures. Some of these animals were incredibly tall, some had sharp teeth, some had huge, long necks—they were the dinosaurs!

Due to the study of fossils, we know the story of living things and of the Earth itself. For example, we know that:

3,600 million years ago, life first appeared on Earth as simple cells.

650 million years ago, the first animal with more than one cell appeared.

360 million years ago, land animals with backbones (vertebrates) appeared.

65 million years ago, dinosaurs became extinct.

0.1 million years ago, Homo sapiens, the human species, was born.

If we made the history of the Earth last for one hour, it would look like this: after the first 20 minutes, the first living things would appear. Then after 55 minutes, dinousaurs would appear. 40 seconds before the end of the hour, Hominoidea (the group of primates that includes apes and humans) would be born, and only when the timer went off at the end of the hour would humans appear.

# Beaks

All birds and some fish and mammals have beaks. These allow them to reach and eat their food easily, and are sometimes used for other things, too.

The beaks of birds have evolved over thousands of years, depending on the food each species eats. By looking at the huge variety of beaks that exist today, from short and small to long and wide, we can understand how this works.

The beak of the red crossbill (Loxia curvirostra) is crossed over at the tips, making it the perfect tool to extract seeds from pine cones.

The toucan's (Ramphastidae) amazing beak developed for a surprising reason: to keep the bird cool in the rainforest! Blood flows to the beak, which carries heat away from the toucan's body, cooling it down.

The shoebill (Balaeniceps rex) has a long, wide beak with a sharp hook on the end. It uses it to hunt large prey, such as eels, snakes, and even baby crocodiles, in the swamps where it lives.

The bird with the longest beak compared to its body is the sword-billed hummingbird (Ensifera ensifera). The beak is almost as heavy as the bird's body. It allows the hummingbird to reach the nectar of particular flowers with very long petals.

The common spoonbill (Platalea leucorodia) has a spoon-shaped beak. It sweeps it from side to side in water to scoop up food such as frogs, fish, and shrimp.

A vulture's hooked beak is specially designed for tearing and chopping dead animals before eating them.

# Defenses

## Shells, prickles, spines, and more...

In this section, we are going to look at how and why some animals have developed ways to protect themselves, helping their species to survive.

Vertebrates have internal skeletons, but many other species have an external skeleton—one that can be seen. This is the case for spiders and many other insects, but also other animals, such as coral.

Animals defend themselves in countless ways.

The pangolin is covered with scaly skin to protect it, and can roll into a ball to defend itself.

The Indian rhinoceros (Rhinoceros unicornis) looks like it is covered in sheets of armor, but this is actually just thick, protective skin.

Hedgehogs haven't changed for 15 million years. Sharp spines on their back help prevent predators from attacking them.

Some mollusks, such as mussels, oysters, and snails, have formed a hard shell made from calcium that protects them.

Turtles are known for their extremely hard shell. The shell is made from bone, which is joined to the turtle's back and ribs and protects it from attacks.

However, the underside of a turtle's body is soft, so it is at risk if it turns upside down or is attacked from underneath.

Some sea turtles have a softer shell that doesn't protect them so well. However, this means they can swim faster to escape predators instead.

# Legs

Vertebrates with four limbs (legs or arms) are called tetrapods. Obvious members of this group include horses, lions, and humans.

Animal limbs come with features of all different shapes and sizes. There are paws with claws, padded feet, suckers, webbed feet, and scales. They can adapt to any function you could imagine—running, jumping, absorbing crash landings, climbing, scratching, or even flying.

However, you might be surprised to know that tetrapods also include whales, bats, birds, and snakes, because they, or their ancestors, have four limbs. It's probably quite hard to imagine whales and snakes (or their relatives) walking on the ground using four legs!

Giraffes (Giraffa camelopardalis) have long, strong legs that help carry their large bodies. However, they are so long that in order to drink, they must bend or open their legs very wide to be able to reach the water in lakes low on the ground.

An octopus has two legs and six arms, called tentacles. They are covered in suckers for gripping.

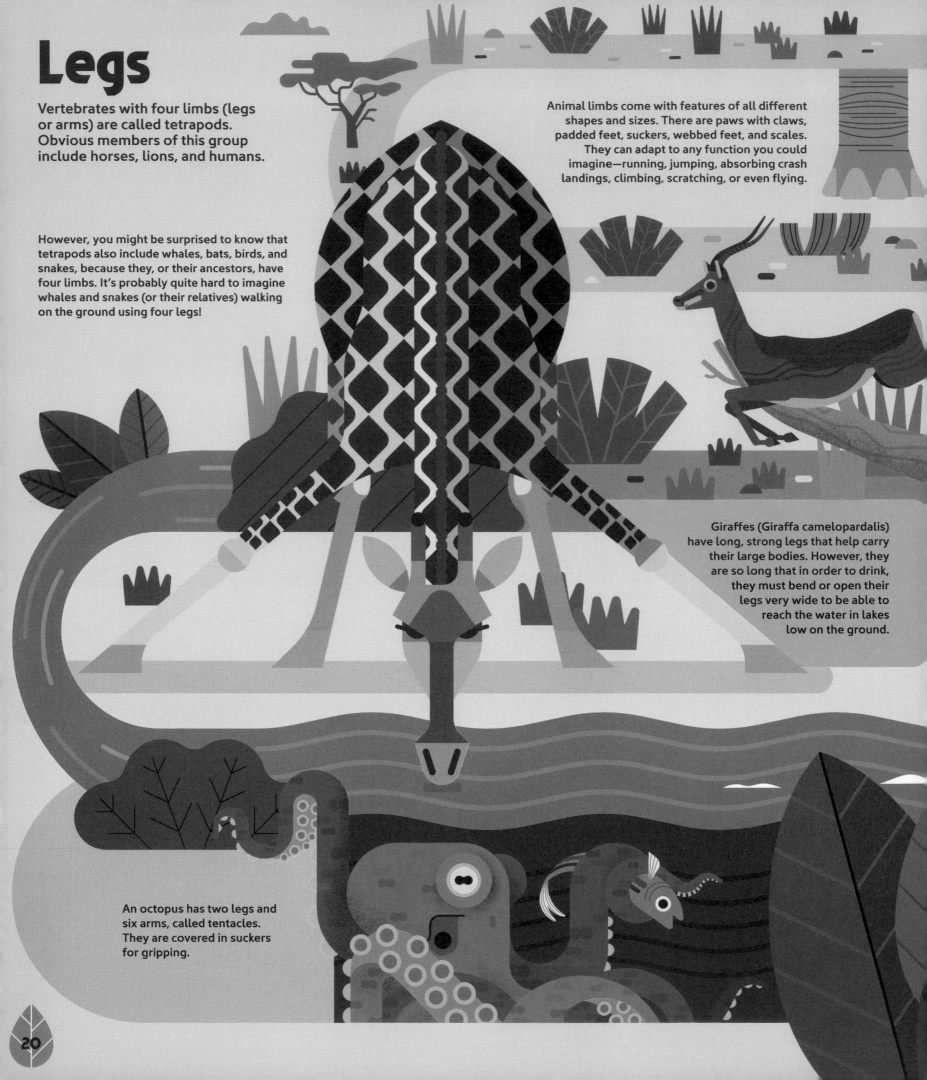

Horses' legs are adapted to run in a straight line. Their bones cannot rotate to allow them to move in circles like humans can. This is because horses originally came from areas without trees or bushes that they might have to dodge around when running away from predators. The fastest way for them to escape was running straight ahead, so they became experts at running that way.

Ostriches are the heaviest of all birds, and that's why they can't fly. Their wings are useless for flying. However, their legs are long, allowing them to run very fast—they can sprint up to 43 mph (70 kph)!

Mammals that live in meadows and are hunted by other mammals have legs designed like springs to help them gain speed quickly. Some of them, such as antelopes, can jump like athletes to escape danger.

The legs of some insects, such as the common water strider (Gerris lacustris), mean they can skate across the surface of water.

The basilisk, a species of lizard, can sprint over water to escape from predators. It has adapted to do this by developing flaps of skin between its toes. The flaps unfurl, slapping against the water to create bubbles of air that keep it from sinking.

Some other species also have suckers on their limbs, such as Peter's disk-winged bat (Thyroptera discifera). This rare species of bat has suckers at the base of its hind feet and thumbs, which allows it to stick to slippery leaves, where it roosts.

Some birds, such as the common blackbird (Turdus merula), are not fully adapted to move on the ground, and hop, rather than walk. However, this is not a problem for these birds – not every animal needs to move in the way humans do.

Each species has developed abilities that are useful to them. What is essential for some animals is totally useless for others.

# Claws

Claws are hard, pointed nails on the hands or feet of some vertebrates. They can be used to cut, attack prey, dig holes, or grip onto things. Claws are often attached to paws, which are feet whose toes can't move separately from each other.

The harpy eagle (Harpia harpyja) is one of the biggest eagles in the world. Its huge claws can reach 6 in (15 cm) long.

Many birds of prey, such as the Spanish imperial eagle (Aquila adalberti) or the peregrine falcon (Falco peregrinus), have very strong claws. They use them to strike their prey and grasp onto it. They can even carry prey through the air.

Not all claws are used to attack, though. For example, iguanas use them to grip onto unsteady surfaces. Another example are chameleons, who live in trees. Their toes are gathered into groups of two, a bit like tongs, and each toe has a sharp claw. This shape helps them hold firmly onto tree branches.

Almost all members of the cat family have paws with retractable claws. This means that most of the time, the claws are hidden in the paws. Cats can then extend them when they want to attack or scratch.

The three-toed sloth (Bradypus) is known for its claws, which are enormous. They are not used to hunt, but to hang from trees, where sloths spends most of their time. When walking, the sloth can also dig its front claws into the ground and use its strong front legs to pull it along.

The giant armadillo (Priodontes maximus) uses its very large, thick, strong front claws to scratch the ground, looking for insects to eat, and to tear into termite mounds. It can also use them to build burrows to shelter or hide from danger. The claw on the third finger of each hand is particularly long.

Bears, like humans, are plantigrade, which means that they walk on the soles of their feet. Their claws are like sharp knives. They can be over 4 in (10 cm) long, depending on the species.

# Colors

The colors you see in nature are not just for decoration! Like so many of the features discussed in this book, they are essential for the survival of many species, and this is all down to evolution.

Some species, such as tigers, have colors that act as camouflage, helping them to blend into their surroundings.

Some butterflies have evolved to have wing patterns that look like the colors and faces of bigger and more dangerous animals. Predators are frightened off, mistaking the butterfly for an animal that could attack or eat them.

Although it's not true that chameleons can change color to completely match their surroundings, they can slightly adjust the darkness or lightness of their skin to blend in with their surroundings. They do change their colors to stand out if they are in danger, to scare off predators. Like many animals, male chameleons can also turn their skin bright colors to attract females.

The European robin (Erithacus rubecula) is a bird with orange-red feathers on its breast. Both males and females have a red spot, which grows larger as the robin gets older, but in male birds the spot is bigger. So scientists believe that the evolution of the red feathers is something to do with a robin's age and sex.

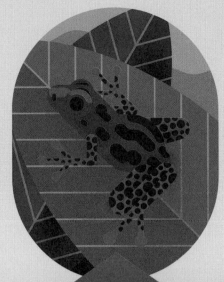

Some animals pretend to be poisonous to confuse predators. For example, the milk snake (Lampropeltis triangulum) isn't venomous, but it has adopted the same yellow, red, and black stripes as its venomous neighbor, the coral snake (Micrurus fulvius). This tricks predators into thinking that it is a dangerous coral snake, and so they leave it alone!

In the underwater world, orange elephant ear sponges (Agelas clathrodes) have a dark orange color to tell predators that they taste bitter and not to eat them.

Some caterpillars, such as the cinnabar moth (Tyria jacobaeae), are yellow and black. Birds avoid them because these colors in nature usually show that something is poisonous.

The golden poison frog (Phyllobates terribilis) contains enough venom to kill two adult humans. Its bright yellow, orange, or green skin signals that it is dangerous.

## Why are feathers colorful?

This question has more than one answer! Some birds have colorful feathers because they eat vegetables that have colored substances in them, called carotenoids. They absorb them from the food and their feathers become red, yellow, or orange. Other foods contain a different substance called melanin, that turns feathers brown or gray. Some bright feather colors, such as iridescent (shining) blue or green don't come from food at all, and are the result of light reflecting off the feathers.

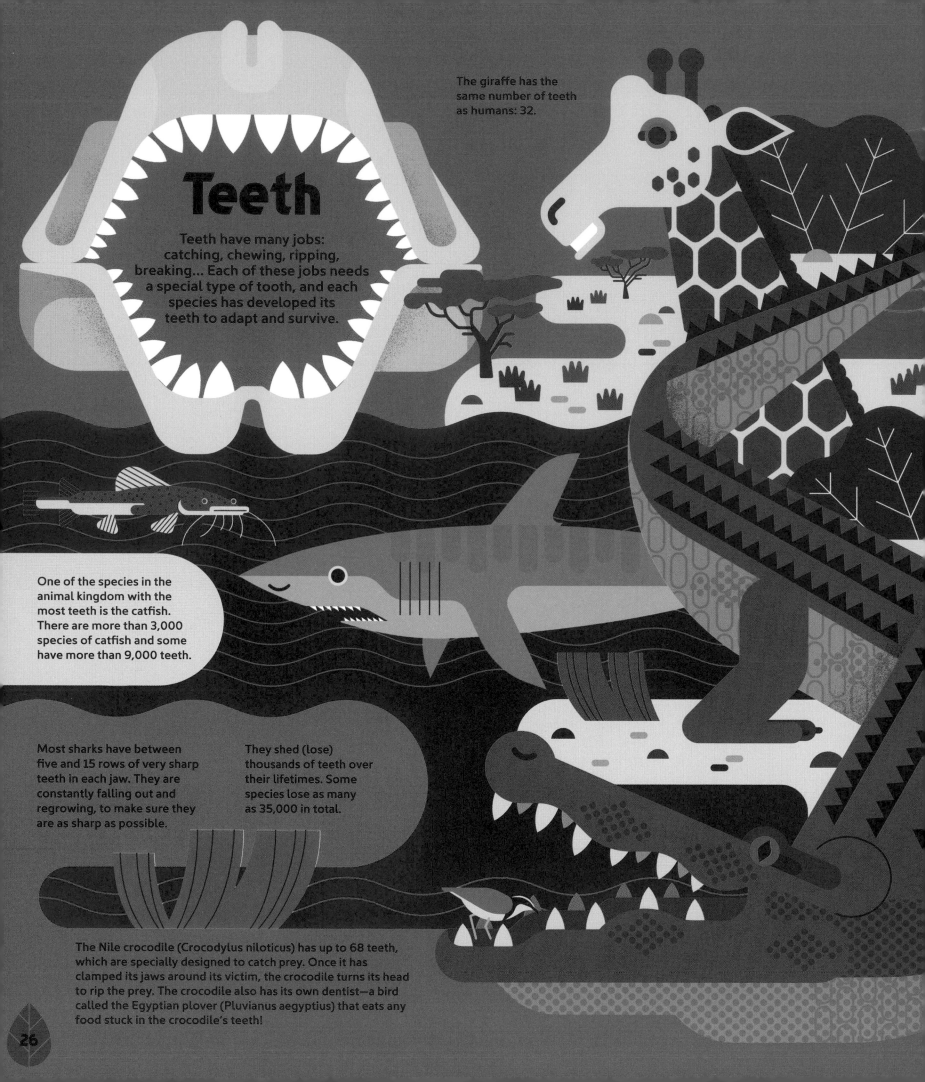

# Teeth

Teeth have many jobs: catching, chewing, ripping, breaking... Each of these jobs needs a special type of tooth, and each species has developed its teeth to adapt and survive.

The giraffe has the same number of teeth as humans: 32.

One of the species in the animal kingdom with the most teeth is the catfish. There are more than 3,000 species of catfish and some have more than 9,000 teeth.

Most sharks have between five and 15 rows of very sharp teeth in each jaw. They are constantly falling out and regrowing, to make sure they are as sharp as possible.

They shed (lose) thousands of teeth over their lifetimes. Some species lose as many as 35,000 in total.

The Nile crocodile (Crocodylus niloticus) has up to 68 teeth, which are specially designed to catch prey. Once it has clamped its jaws around its victim, the crocodile turns its head to rip the prey. The crocodile also has its own dentist—a bird called the Egyptian plover (Pluvianus aegyptius) that eats any food stuck in the crocodile's teeth!

Not all animals have teeth. Some whales have brushlike bristles instead. The blue whale (Balaenoptera musculus) sifts water through bristly filters called baleen, which catch tiny sea creatures, such as krill and plankton, for it to eat.

Teeth aren't just useful for eating. They can be used to communicate, too. Many mammals show their teeth, but this isn't just to smile like humans do...

Elephants' tusks are large teeth used for fighting, lifting things, and gathering food.

Many venomous snakes have fangs, which are specialized teeth used to bite prey and inject them with venom to kill them.

Some creatures, such as mandrill monkeys (Mandrillus sphinx), show their teeth when they are angry. When chimpanzees (Pan troglodytes) "smile," they are showing that they are scared, not happy.

# Feathers

Feathers grow out of skin and are made of a substance called keratin. This is the same material found in human hair and fingernails. From studying fossils, some scientists believe that feathers first developed on the legs of fast-running animals to help them keep their balance. Later, they became used for flying. Another thought is that animals developed wing feathers for gliding between trees—but no one knows for sure.

Even though birds come in all different shapes and sizes, most flying birds have the types of feathers below. The primaries, on the tip of the wing, are the largest feathers. They push the bird through the air and control its direction as it flies.

1. Primaries
2. Primary coverts
3. Alula
4. Secondaries
5. Greater secondary coverts
6. Median coverts
7. Lesser coverts
8. Tertials
9. Axillars

A feather's structure is complicated. Its central part is a long, solid tube called the rachis. The rachis joins to the calamus, which is a hollow tube, and is where the feather attaches to a bird's skin. The vane and barb are the soft, fluffy parts of the feather.

Rachis    Vane    Barbs    Calamus

Tail feathers are called rectrices. They steer the bird through the air and allow it to brake when it is flying. Birds that glide through the air are especially good at using these feathers.

## How do birds stay dry in the water?

Birds that dive or float on the surface of the water have a special way of staying dry. It would be very difficult to survive if they were soaking wet all the time—this would make them too heavy to fly away from danger. These birds release a waterproof oil near their tails, which they spread all over their bodies with their beaks. It means that water will just slide off their feathers, rather than sinking in and making them wet.

## Birds that can't fly

Thanks to evolution, many birds have lost their ability to fly over time. They have found better ways of escaping predators. Some birds, such as penguins, have turned their wings into fins to help them swim. Others, such as emus, have become experts in running so their legs have become stronger. Some that live in isolated places, such as islands, with no predators at all, stopped flying completely.

# Hair

Mammals' skin is protected by hair, which is also called fur in non-human mammals. Hair can provide a lot of information about evolution and how animals have adapted. It protects them from bad weather and prevents them getting scratched by plants or other animals.

Many animals, such as some wolves, change their hair to suit different seasons. Their hair is long and thin in summer when the weather is hotter, but it grows longer to keep them warm in winter.

Many pigs, such as wild boars (Sus scrofa), have long and rough hair called bristle. This is perfect for protecting their skin in places such as woods which are full of prickly plants, rough roots, and sharp branches.

Otters are great swimmers. Their fur is thick and can adapt to water. When they swim, the hairs create a barrier that prevents water from touching their skin so the otters don't get cold.

The fur of some hunters, such as the tiger (Panthera tigris) and the leopard (Panthera pardus), is colored and patterned in a way that hides them in their environment. This way, they can't be seen by their prey as the hunters approach them.

A panda's black and white coat acts as camouflage in its environment. The white fur blends into the snowy background of its cold mountain home, and the black fur looks like the shadows of trees.

Some mammals have very little hair or no hair at all. A breed of cat (Felis catus), called the sphynx cat, appears to be hairless, although it has fine hairs all over its body.

# Scales

Scales are thick, hard pieces of skin that protect animals. Many small scales overlap each other to allow scaly creatures to move easily. You might expect fish and reptiles to have scales, but some other animals have them, too.

There are different types of scales, depending on what they are going to be used for. The scales of fish, reptiles, birds, mammals, and insects are usually quite different from one another. This is because they have evolved in different ways. Look at the sardine and the snake on this page. How are their scales different?

Insects such as butterflies and moths have tiny scales on their wings, which give them their beautiful color. Their scales will fall away if anything touches them.

## Do birds have scales?

Yes! Unlike butterflies, they aren't found on their wings but on their legs and feet. For example, the claws of the Steller's sea eagle (Haliaeetus pelagicus) are covered in yellow scales. In the past, scientists thought that these scales were the same as reptile scales, but they now know that they have evolved from birds' feathers.

Many different types of animals have scales, including some mammals. For example, mice have tiny scales on their tails, and anteaters are covered with big protective scales.

# Surprising finds

Scientists who study evolution often have to think like detectives, searching for clues that can help them understand evolution better. Some of the things that they find are surprising. On this page, you'll find a few curious cases of evolution.

## Vestigial organs

In some animals, scientists have discovered body parts that once had a job but that are no longer needed. These are called vestigial organs.

It might be hard to believe, but ancestors of the whale used to walk on the ground. We know this from looking at four-legged animals, who all have a set of bones that connects their legs to their body, called the pelvis. Whales and some other sea-living mammals still have elements of a pelvis, which doesn't work any more. This is a clue that they once had legs, suggesting they haven't always lived in water.

# Convergent evolution

Another curious case are animals that aren't related but have developed similar features due to evolution. This process is called convergent evolution.

An example is the extinct Tasmanian wolf (Thylacinus cynocephalus). This animal was related to koalas and kangaroos, but its carnivorous (meat-filled) diet meant that it evolved to look more like a wolf.

Many fish have an air bladder—a sac they fill with gas to float in water. It is possible that for their ancestors, this was a type of lung that they had in order to breathe. This may show that fish once breathed air like humans. However, it's also possible that lungs evolved from air bladders.

Hedgehogs, echidnas, and porcupines are similar in that they all have spines, but they aren't related to one another.

Bats and dolphins are from very different animal families, but they both use echolocation. This is where they send out a sound that bounces off an object, and listen to the echo. This tells the animal where the object is.

# Fins

Fins are special limbs used by underwater animals to move through water. Some water animals evolved into land animals over time, and their fins became legs. At the same time, some land animals, such as dolphins, evolved into water animals, and their legs evolved into fins to live in the water.

Fish and some marine mammals, such as whales and dolphins, have different types of fins. Each of them has a different role to play.

Some types of fins come in pairs. Pectoral fins can be found just behind a fish's gills. They control the fish's movement up and down and side to side. Pelvic fins, underneath the fish's body, help it swim steadily.

Pectoral fins

Pelvic fins

Some types of fins don't come in pairs, although fish sometimes have more than one of them. A shark has two dorsal fins on its back. They keep the shark upright in the water.

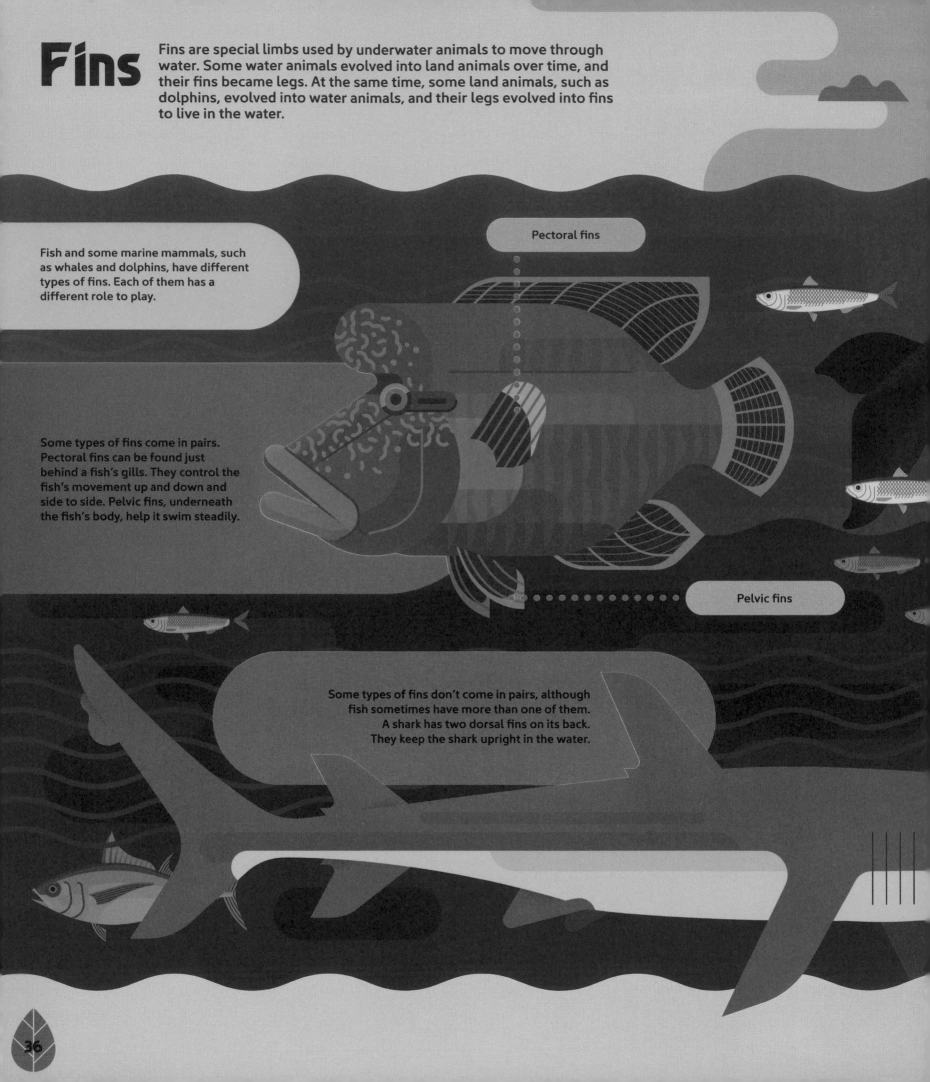

The dorsal fin of a male orca (Orcinus orca) is as tall as a person. It can help keep the orca steady as it swims at high speeds. It is also used to keep it cool.

The tail fin is called the caudal fin. It is essential for swimming. There are many different types of caudal fin depending on how each species moves. They can be vertical or horizontal, simple or quite complex.

Sardines have a short, vertical tail fin that is almost divided into two parts.

Mosquito fish (Gambusia affinis) have a wide, rounded caudal fin, a bit like a fan.

Many fish also have an anal fin.

Some types of fins are unique to just one type of fish. For example, some tuna, such as the bigeye tuna (Thunnus obesus), have small fins all along their back, stretching from the dorsal fin to the caudal fin.

# The curious case of the evolution of Fingers

**WHALE**   **FROG**   **HORSE**

Here, we'll look at how fingers have changed. Evolution of the finger bones depends on how useful they are and why they are used. When they are not used, many animals lose some or all of them!

As you can see, the fingers of cetaceans such as whales are hidden in their flippers and will probably eventually disappear completely. Some flying animals have kept their fingers in different ways—bat fingers have grown long, and are attached to the membrane of their wings, giving them incredible control over their movements. Most birds have either lost their fingers or made them smaller.

Most dogs have five fingers on their front paws and four on their back paws. The fifth finger, called the dewclaw, is usually only present in dogs that are made for running and jumping. The dewclaw (like a thumb) digs into the ground and helps to keep them steady.

Did you know that some animals have adapted their fingers to be able to carry all of their weight on a single finger? Animals such as horses have only kept one finger, with a nail—their hooves—on each leg to walk on.

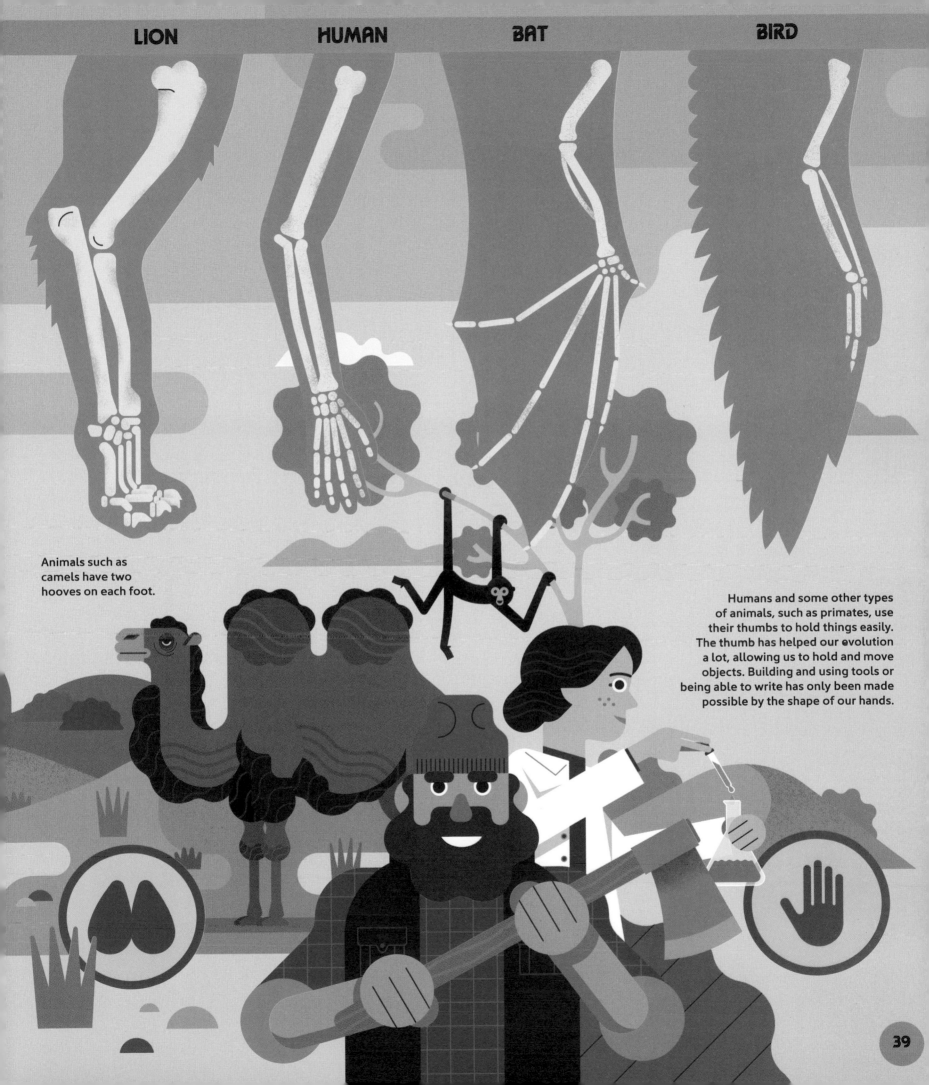

LION HUMAN BAT BIRD

Animals such as camels have two hooves on each foot.

Humans and some other types of animals, such as primates, use their thumbs to hold things easily. The thumb has helped our evolution a lot, allowing us to hold and move objects. Building and using tools or being able to write has only been made possible by the shape of our hands.

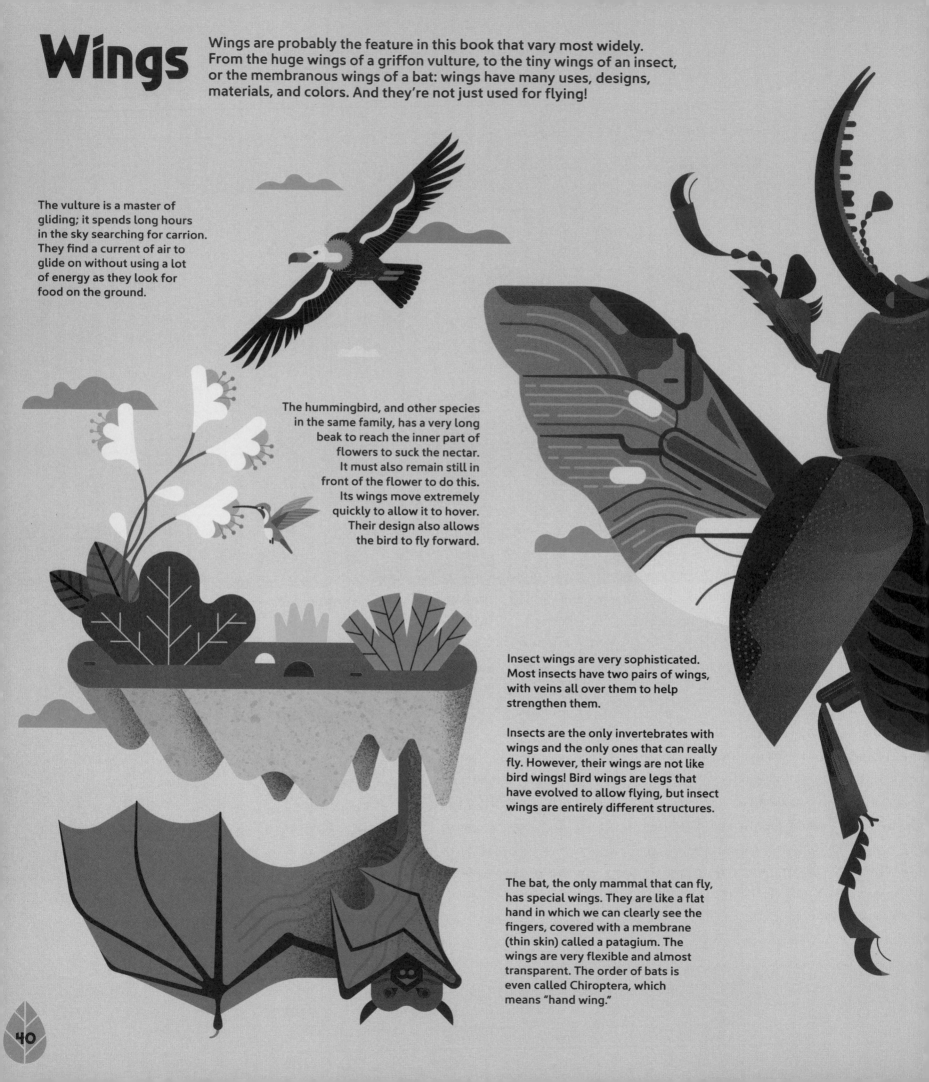

# Wings

Wings are probably the feature in this book that vary most widely. From the huge wings of a griffon vulture, to the tiny wings of an insect, or the membranous wings of a bat: wings have many uses, designs, materials, and colors. And they're not just used for flying!

The vulture is a master of gliding; it spends long hours in the sky searching for carrion. They find a current of air to glide on without using a lot of energy as they look for food on the ground.

The hummingbird, and other species in the same family, has a very long beak to reach the inner part of flowers to suck the nectar. It must also remain still in front of the flower to do this. Its wings move extremely quickly to allow it to hover. Their design also allows the bird to fly forward.

Insect wings are very sophisticated. Most insects have two pairs of wings, with veins all over them to help strengthen them.

Insects are the only invertebrates with wings and the only ones that can really fly. However, their wings are not like bird wings! Bird wings are legs that have evolved to allow flying, but insect wings are entirely different structures.

The bat, the only mammal that can fly, has special wings. They are like a flat hand in which we can clearly see the fingers, covered with a membrane (thin skin) called a patagium. The wings are very flexible and almost transparent. The order of bats is even called Chiroptera, which means "hand wing."

Lepidopterans (butterflies) have tiny, colorful scales covering their wings. Caddis flies (a species related to butterflies and moths) have hair on their wings.

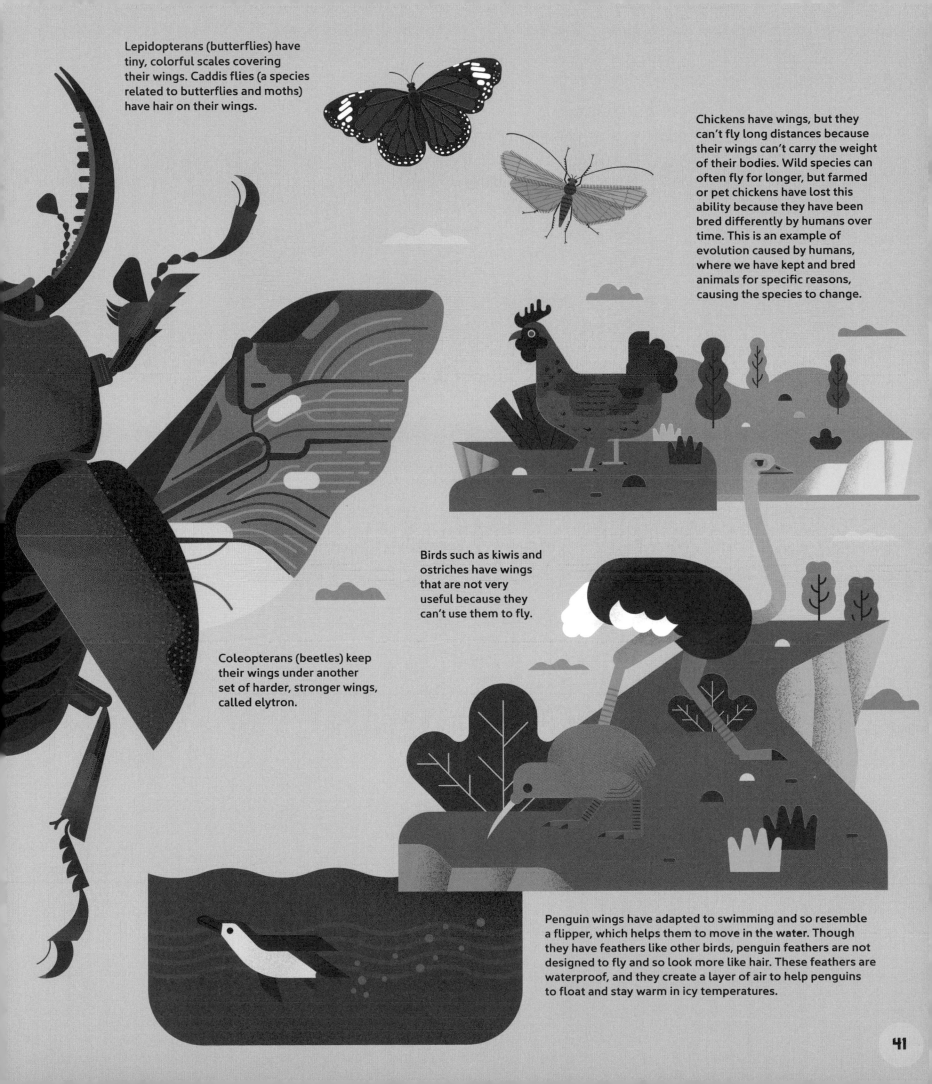

Chickens have wings, but they can't fly long distances because their wings can't carry the weight of their bodies. Wild species can often fly for longer, but farmed or pet chickens have lost this ability because they have been bred differently by humans over time. This is an example of evolution caused by humans, where we have kept and bred animals for specific reasons, causing the species to change.

Birds such as kiwis and ostriches have wings that are not very useful because they can't use them to fly.

Coleopterans (beetles) keep their wings under another set of harder, stronger wings, called elytron.

Penguin wings have adapted to swimming and so resemble a flipper, which helps them to move in the water. Though they have feathers like other birds, penguin feathers are not designed to fly and so look more like hair. These feathers are waterproof, and they create a layer of air to help penguins to float and stay warm in icy temperatures.

# Mr. Linnaeus

## and his obsession with organization

More than 300 years ago, scientists and normal people alike were passionate about the ways of nature, but didn't know how to classify (group) living things to understand their origins. They faced several challenges. First, what name should be given to each living thing so that it could be recognized in all languages? Second, how could living things be scientifically organized?

Swedish botanist Charles Linnaeus provided the solution: he created a classification system for all living things (plants and animals), and he also suggested giving each species a scientific name in Latin, to avoid confusion between different languages.

He proposed that similar species could be grouped into a genus. These genera would, in turn, be grouped into families, and families with similar characteristics grouped into orders, then classes, then phyla, and then, finally, in kingdoms. It seems complicated, but it becomes clearer when you look at examples. See on the opposite page how Linnaeus would classify a cat, for example.

You'll be able to understand why a cat and a lion are related, and you will also be able to clearly see which animals are not related! The cat may be linked to many different types of animal, but a bird, such as a parrot, has a different ancient ancestor. Linnaeus' classification system also helps us to understand evolution.

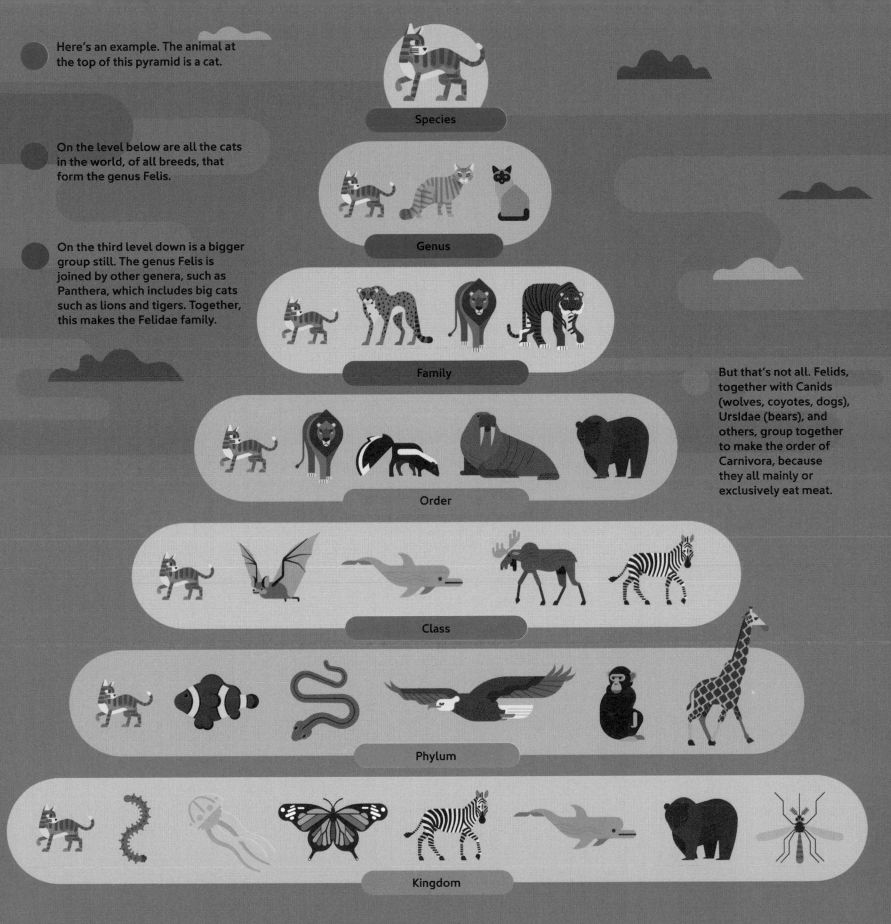

Here's an example. The animal at the top of this pyramid is a cat.

**Species**

On the level below are all the cats in the world, of all breeds, that form the genus Felis.

**Genus**

On the third level down is a bigger group still. The genus Felis is joined by other genera, such as Panthera, which includes big cats such as lions and tigers. Together, this makes the Felidae family.

**Family**

But that's not all. Felids, together with Canids (wolves, coyotes, dogs), Ursidae (bears), and others, group together to make the order of Carnivora, because they all mainly or exclusively eat meat.

**Order**

**Class**

**Phylum**

**Kingdom**

Carnivora, along with Rodentia, Primates, and others, belong to the class of Mammals, because they suckle (breastfeed) their young.

Mammals, Fish, Reptiles, and Amphibians have a spine, making them vertebrates. Vertebrates all belong to the phylum Chordata.

Chordates, along with insects (Arthropods), shellfish, and more, are part of the animal kingdom.

Each category contains the previous one, plus others.

# Glossary

**ability**
Skill to do something

**adapt**
How a living thing changes its appearance or behavior to better fit in with its environment

**adaptation**
Way in which an animal or a plant becomes better-suited to its habitat

**ancestor**
Ancient relative of a living thing

**antennae**
Pair of feelers, located near the front of an insect's head, that it can use to sense its surroundings

**arthropod**
Group of invertebrates with a tough outer skeleton and a body divided into segments

**botanist**
Scientist who studies plants

**bred**
When an animal is brought up in a specific environment or way

**camouflage**
Colors or patterns on an animal's skin, fur, or feathers that help it blend in with the environment

**cell**
Tiny parts of the body of a living thing that carry out different jobs, such as fighting infection

**cetacean**
Group of water mammals, usually living in the sea, that includes whales, dolphins, and porpoises

**class**
Group of living things based on their general features

**crustacean**
An invertebrate with jointed legs and often a hard shell or exoskeleton, such as a crab, shrimp, or wood louse

**family**
Group of the same kind of animals, such as dogs, cats, or tarantulas

**gene**
Sections of DNA that carry instructions for how the body looks

**generation**
Group of living things that are of a similar age, and usually related; for example, brothers and sisters are one generation and their parents are another

**genus**
Animals in the same groups that are very closely related, such as dogs and wolves

**invertebrate**
Animal that does not have a backbone

**isolated**
Far away from other places, buildings, or people

## lens
Part of the eye that helps to focus light

## limb
Arm or leg of an animal, or a bird's wing

## mammal
Vertebrate animal that is fed by milk from its mother when it is young

## membrane
Thin skin or layer of material

## mollusk
Invertebrate that usually has a shell and often lives in damp habitats

## order
Group of closely-related families

## organ
Body part that has a certain job; for example, the heart, which pumps blood

## perceive
Become aware of or identify something using the senses

## phylum
Group of animals with the same body features

## plantigrade
When an animal walks on the soles of their feet

## predator
Animal that hunts other living animals for food

## prey
Animal that is hunted by another animal for food

## primate
Group of mammals, which includes monkeys

## retina
Part of the eye that receives light

## retractable
Able to be pulled back in

## specialized
Adapted to do a specific job

## species
Specific types of animals or plants with shared features that can mate and produce young together

## tetrapod
Four-limbed animal

## venom
Harmful substance released by an animal or plant that may be deadly if injected into the skin, by a sting or fangs

## vertebrate
Animals having a backbone or spine and a brain enclosed within a skull, such as mammals and birds

# Index

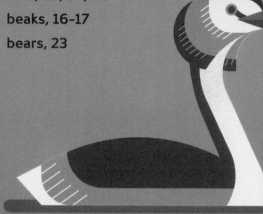